IT MATTERS NOW

Sue P.

IT

MATTERS

NOW

S. P. Joshi

Matador
9 Priory Business Park
Kibworth Beauchamp
Leicestershire LE8 0RX, UK
Tel: (+44) 116 279 2299
Fax: (+44) 116 279 2277
Email: books@troubador.co.uk
Web: www.troubador.co.uk/matador

ISBN 978-1784621-537

British Library Cataloguing in Publication Data.
A catalogue record for this book is available from the British Library.

Typeset in Aldine by Troubador Publishing Ltd
Printed and bound in the UK by TJ International, Padstow, Cornwall

Matador is an imprint of Troubador Publishing Ltd

This book is dedicated to my parents
for their wisdom, strength and inspiration.

❧ ACKNOWLEDGEMENTS ❧

Jeremy Thompson and his publishing team for their support and clarity throughout.

Dr. Vanita Sharma for encouraging me to write and publish this book.

Suni who has worked in the background despite her busy schedules.

Dr. Gwen Bonner who made a positive difference to my life.

❧ CONTENTS ❧

⟫ INTRODUCTION ⟪

I love walking and it's when I reflect on things. At times I like to talk to people from all walks of life or simply be in the moment. We all change in our life journeys on the paths we take. And the choices we make can influence us whether we're being positive or negative about life.

I have worked in the therapeutic field of psychiatry and psychology for over twenty years. If there's anything I've learnt, it's what matters to you now. I felt the time had come for shared learning so I am writing this book in a non-judgemental way. Life has taught me some harsh lessons but these have also been valuable to me; helping me when I needed to be strong.

Writing this book also made me reflect on my spiritual journey.

One day I desperately needed to be heard. At the time the person was unavailable. Whatever the matter was it had brought me to my knees. It was a cry from my soul. Sometime later, I felt as if I was being guided by something powerful. I got up and returned to my room writing down everything on paper. My pen flowed with ease and the words came easily. The very next day I read the pile of papers I'd written and, to my surprise, everything was in poems.

I was asked to contribute something from a therapist's point of view for World Mental Health Day. I contributed a piece of writing from the drafts of this book. It led to much interest on the day and I promised to add the piece in this published book.

For the reader I've used the word 'I' for the voice.

∞ BELIEVE IN YOURSELF ∞

Don't let others sidetrack you
in to thinking
'You're being foolish.'
Nothing's ever futile.

Whatever's your intent
do it with your heart's
content.

Aim for success,
because nothing
in life's so
stress free.

❦ YOU'RE NOT ALONE ❧

Don't lose touch
with family and friends
who love you so much.

And if I could
I'd run-a-mile.

To get your smile
back on.

✑ RIVALRY ✑

There was silence
between us when the
two of us came to see you.

Your words gushed out
thick and fast.

'We decided to pick on you.'
Shell-shocked and numb
we stood as dumb.

What a load of gobbledegook.

To think, you served a
left hook.
Made, no sense.
'Who were we?'

Stood like cowards,
but wanted to flee.
Drove us home,
but didn't come in.
Now we won't
give you a look-in.

❧ INSPIRED ❦

The sun
will shine.
It's
in your
belief.

Sometimes
inspiration comes
from the simplest
of things

I have
my health.
What more
can I
ask for?

✑ BULLYING ✑

'EVERYONE', knows 'SOMEONE' who's 'A
BULLY' or 'BEEN BULLIED'.

'A bully' –
or 'bullies'.

Have a
canny streak.
When others they seek as weak,
and are discreet when they greet you
with open arms.

They'll
pick on others and be
cruel and unkind, and have
someone in mind to latch onto.

It causes worry when
you can't work, sleep or play
and want to
keep bully or bullies at bay.

People watch and see
and keep
a close ear to the ground,
for bully, bullies or victim.

Bullies want to be discreet
when there's nowhere to run.

'Less people who know, the better,'
They say.

'The more people who know, the better,'
We say.

✑ ANGER ✐

It was
like a spark
in an engine, and I'd
lark about.

But soon
it turned to
rage and fury.
That left everyone, in the
dark –
where it'd kill or
cause injury.

ANGER

Before
anger controls you,
control your anger.
Or, it'll spread
inside of you, and engulf
you.

ANGER

Slowly it simmered.
Like a kettle,
waiting to come to
boil.

ANGER

People fled in tears
when you'd lash out,
with your tongue.

ANGER

We were having a battle of words
so, you'd let go of your pride and
pomposity.

Now,
you're doing their
head-in, and they simply
want you to heed.

Now
A
Momentous
Breath.

Yesterday's
A
Memory.

And
Tomorrow's
Faraway.

~ THANKS A BUNCH ~

We played
in the same
neighbourhood.

And, mums were
close at hand
when we popped
into each other's
houses.

We'd make daisy chains
for fun, and go for a run.
Giggled we did at
silly things but
our friendship was a
test of time.

Now with
children and grandchildren
our stories we told, many
times.

'I wish I had a friend like you, Nan.'
I burst with pride knowing my
best friend.

❧ SUCCESS ❧

Whether
success is
wealth or status,
it's a
personal thing.

Whether
to aim for the top
and never stop.

Whether
to
count your blessings
and
feel blessed.

Whether
to have
materialistic things and
all kinds of bling.

Whether,
'There's a point?'
And
want success

handed on a plate.
Whether
to care
more or less –
regardless.

Or to
just believe
in yourself,
when
no other
will.

Buzz around you did,
and I
followed my hunch.

Soon it became a
game of 'two halves'.

You played one against the
other and secured their places
when,
their names you never stopped
to call, endlessly.

It was noted.

There was a rift,
in the division and across the
board.
Eyebrows were raised that
followed in silences.

I didn't give
'two monkeys' when others
you had on a wild goose
chase.

You couldn't
hide from yourself and others
as to
who you really are.

And when your mask
did drop
they saw you
for
what you really are.
How bizarre.

DOMESTIC VIOLENCE

You grew up, with your dream
or so it seemed, that your
Prince Charming would
sweep you off your feet.

To think,
you'd be there through the
years –
you truly
believed in.

Reality was
such a different thing and not
out of this
world.

At first, your perfect dream.

But slowly,
you saw the cracks and knew
it wasn't the real thing.
To you it surprised,
this could –
even be.

As if
a dramatised play, you both
displayed.
Hard to scrutinise if a lie, you'd
both implied for all to see.

He was a stranger to them
but they saw him as a perfect
gentleman.
Convincing he'd be that left you
with such unease.

You 'knew'.
'Jeckyll and Hyde'.
You weren't blind.

Sly as a fox, you he'd coax
using his box of 'tricks'.
He was so slimy and for all
you knew, it was a matter of
time.
'You could be dead'.
That was in your head,
all the time.

It sent alarm bells ringing
when the fear in you scared you,
and that he controlled you –
behind closed doors, in front of
others and even the children.

You'd run out of places to hide,
and to keep children out of sight
before he –
'hooks you'.

Running scared not knowing
what he'd toss or who'd be next.
Or, who'd be flung across the floor
and even bashed or smashed,
which made you jump out of your
skin to even think of the pain.

You had to find a way out.
But not leave the children
behind.

He
'lost' your post, and cut off the
line.
Now so
out of touch with the outside
world, with family and friends
you missed.

No more fight left in you, and
days were numbered.
But you had to, stand on your
own two feet, to find the
strength to carry on.

Whether you're an adult or a
child, you cannot always
give as good as you get.

Now.
An expert to hide the bruises,
you'd never run out of excuses.

You wanted to be 'safe as houses'
where you could sleep and not
weep.

And have family and friends
you knew, well.

YOU WON'T BREAK MY COURAGE

Others do not see,
when you
mislead them
about me.

And now,
they'll be sorry.

They
trusted you, and not me.

✑ UNDERSTANDING ✑

Never doubt.

Technology's in and not out.

Money spent, thick and fast
and now you weep, it didn't last.

Worried sick, to pay the banks
and loan sharks, breathing down
your neck.

Every generation, a mystery
and with history.

But, a concern
if we don't earn.

⟩ DEAR SIS ⟨

The intensity
is unbearable.

There's no reason
put forward to
justify yourself.

And
the stillness between us
is not of peace.

I won't lie.
When you're
all I have,
even money
can't buy.

❧ HOPES AND DREAMS (PHD) ❧

It's your hope and dream.
And if you believe and care
and don't build castles in the air,
anything's possible.

When others prodded and teased you
and doubted you,
when they were negative,
but it gave you incentive.

Surrounded by your work,
and long hours you put in
when you wanted to,
chuck it all in.

With yourself you'd fight,
when frustration crept in,
and snappy and cranky
you'd become.

22

And run down didn't help
when you became angry.
You couldn't believe it
came, the time it did.

Finally, you'd heard the words, PHD.

⤳ RUMOURS ⤳

A worry or apprehension
or 'something' to question.
Every face tells a story.

Don't get drawn into
Chinese whispers
where you'd applaud
their every spoken word.

If you care about every rumour
in time it'll deafen your ears for
years to come.

We've all been there.
When we can't believe
what we've heard and seen.
Who'd lie through their
back teeth
just to be in.

Some won't.
Point the finger at themselves
when others they seek out –
who aren't there to defend
themselves in reality.

I, just
want you to understand
and to me be kind.
And not
turn the other cheek as – if
I'm blind.

I cannot do it
on my own.
So, please don't
make me feel alone.

It
takes all kinds –
please,
keep that in mind.

IT'S NOT RUBBISH (RECYLING)

Some won't touch it or
make a fuss.
End of the day,
IT'S YOUR RUBBISH.

Week by week, in your street
your bags and bins standing regimental,
and influential on 'collection days'.

The, rubbish men out there
love the job, they do.
But see all that you'd left
and that's a tale to tell.

The word on the street's
'RECYCLING'.

A matter so huge,
affecting worldwide.
Now there's climate change,
carbon footprint and emissions.

So, make the location with each
identification, and follow
strict tracking but, no slacking
because you're backing
'RECYCLING'.
There's a container for
bottles, paper, wood or glass.

Just ask in your neighbourhood
if you've misunderstood.

Global warming and how
frantic is the Antarctic now?

We need to care, for generations to come
and not end, with barren land.

❧ HAPPY NEW YEAR ❧
❧ (AND THE REST) ❧

The
build up was there,
with two days to go
and whatever you'd wished
for,
I wish you well.

Hope was in, and new goals set.

End of year, flu's here.

Sick of a runny nose
and time off for bed rest.

People see red, when their
at work and you're asleep, in bed.
Want you to come in, so
they'd check if it's genuine.

They guess you're out partying
or busy with purchases in the sale.
They say they're loyal, but you've no choice,
and let it ride.

❧ WHO DO YOU ❧
❧ THINK YOU ARE? ❧

I couldn't
just stand and listen
to your voice.

You didn't care,
how you spoke to me
and 'never' by my name.

I tried in vain to correct you
and even to look at you.
But,
you couldn't look me in the eye
when I wanted to
see eye to eye.

Be pleasant, when you
never know
the sort of day
one's had.

❧ GAMES ☙

End of term.
Casual wear and out there,
no school books to carry
and no uniform to wear.

There was a tomboy, amongst us.
Did nothing wrong but wanted to
play football with us.

No gift or panache
but we played each match,
with true sportsmanship.

We'd gush, with the adrenaline rush
and run end to end, to strike a goal.

Flick the ball, toss it or bounce
against the wall, we loved it all.

But when, street lights were lit
there was panic and havoc
when I had to leave, on the
double.
Some would grunt or tut when
so close we were to win.

A rumble in my belly and legs feel like jelly,
when I tried to hurry.
At the door, I froze.
'What took you so long?'

Nothing left to say,
not the first.

And now I'm grounded,
for how long,
I can't say!

∽ JUST ONE DAY ∾

I just
want a day
to myself.

Endless tasks from dawn to dusk.
A lifestyle so cramped, no time
to be still.

No sooner do I turn the key,
to make my house entry
they're all down and around me.
All speaking at once, and I've
no time to catch my breath or
take off my shoes in the process.

I fled the room so fast, just to
clear my head.

All busy with their gadgets, and things to do or
say to one another.

I'm doing the work for two, when they
think I'm the 'butler' and the 'waitress'
all rolled into one.
When will we ever sit and talk to
one another without all these gadgets?

They carry on regardless with their DVDs and
TVs, laptops and computers, browsing or
emails, Facebook, texting, Twitter and Skype –
Oh! What a hype!
Now, I can't use the landline as well.

Endless programmes on TV, and laptops to
record and now constant worry,
if there's room for more.

They're down so fast, like vultures.
No chance to grab a bite, but –
I tell them.

'I'm away for a day.'

They're shocked and screamed,
couldn't believe their ears.

'You're running a fever. Sleep on it.'

'What a sick gimmick.'

They've had a good run for their money and now, they'll have to chip in.

⤚ DEPRESSION ⤙

We
cannot avoid depression,
when it's hidden
to avoid reality.

Be quick to seek
professional help –
as a guide.

For hope to be
and not –
darkness be.

Let's not stigmatise
and realise –
to live in a world
we need to be seen.

ᕙ I'M WORTH IT ᕦ

Because
There can never be
two of me.

⤶ HOPES AND DREAMS ⤷
⤶ (PEAK) ⤷

As if,
a mountain to climb,
you had your mindset and goal set.

Keep others in sight
and not slip or fall
behind.

Focus and concentrate, at
all times.
But don't let doubt set in when
concentration's low.

Draw on
strength and courage
in the belief you can.

Mark your time and days
as each goal you pass.

With numbness and pain,
there's no time to complain
when you need time to
gain.

At your peak.

❧ XMAS AND RECESSION ☙

Maybe
two thousand and eight,
when people quickly learnt
things were changing fast.

To think,
'NO ONE' saw
recession coming.

Questions flew about,
to understand why
people in the trade
didn't work it out.

Now, all eyes
on the Stock Exchange and Wall
Street, and some grit their teeth.

Banks went down and sank
in the river bank.

Shops had 'mark downs'
to pull the punters in,
hoping the gamble will
pay off.

At the end of day, they'd
check their registers and tills,
if scores didn't match
with every batch, losses were
high where doors closed
and people were unemployed.

Even in times like these,
people show their
generosity and kindness.

Thank you.

ᦞ WEIGHT ᦞ

Diabetes.
On the increase, and you
it won't please.

Now that
we've become a
nation of expanded waists and
bigger sizes...

It brings trouble, on the double
with soaring BMIs.

But please,
don't judge when
all you have to do
is be in
your skinny jeans.

When a lifetime I'd spent
on gym equipment, even on
memberships.

But I was in denial
and often called
truce.

So, my weight shot up
along with my BMI,
and I couldn't fit
in my jeans but, marked
my skin 'SORE'.

Off, I went to
Weightwatchers
and, so happy
to be weighed in.

∾ MUM ∾

For truth to be found,
it has to be voiced.
But both staying strong
and stand their ground.

There was a time
when there was such devotion
and now neither will budge
when both hold a grudge.

Why?
Dig up the past. It's breaking
your heart.

When together you'd grown,
and held each other with a
touch at the fingertips.

You pray she has, a place to stay
and take care of herself, and not
run scared.

Your eyes filled with tears.

'A privilege not many have'.
You run downstairs to open the door,
and see your missing child, standing there.

Hugs, so spontaneous.

'Come home to stay Mum.'

'You were right all along Mum.'

Now.

'Let me take care
of you, Mum.'

✑ STRESSING ✑

What's wrong with us?
We
carry on and drive ourselves into
the ground
to accomplish 'all' in one day.

Stress effects us all in many ways,
and end up under pressure and emotional
strain.
Can't chill and worry, one minute
to the next.

Competition's high, with no guarantees
of work – every door shut in your
face, when so many apply and you
say, 'Why, not I?'

Even to have a job, there's constant
worry for some, that you're not unemployed.

Do your best and even take
work home.

On the go we eat, no time
for rest.

Children and babies
to care for.
Let's remember, we need
to talk to one another,
even if technologies are best.

Remember
the quiet ones
who are lost
in the background.

∾ DAD ∾

We laughed and cried,
at times bursting
with pride.

Values and respect,
to never forget.

Right from wrong,
and tough discipline
and you'd always explain
why.

Now.

Children and grandchildren
of my own,

I understand.
Dad.

But, a hug
from my dad
I miss most.

∾ COME HOME ∾

I don't want
anything grand or bland
but for you to understand.
The simple gestures don't
need to cost the earth.
And, once in a while I
wish you'd be on
Planet Earth.

Constant complaining,
of jetlag and time changes
and now,
you've ended up chasing
suitcases.

I wonder
what you're up to.
          or
is there someone?

To have you around
means the world
to me,
when you'll be
beside me.

✑ LINE OF COMMUNICATION ✎

Blood's thicker than water.
We know.
Families should be there
for one another.
But when the phone calls decrease
to endless excuses slowly,
you'd become two strangers
from then on.

If there's any chance, of hope
to end it amicably you want to
reflect on time.

To voice, you miss them.

It's beyond belief to put
limitations on themselves
and others.
After all people come and go
and even the egocentrics
will pretend it's about them,
to think, no other they'll need.

Some, so quick to break ties off.
As if a card to swipe, when they
want to wipe you out, clean.
Then make you plead with them
'It wasn't them'.

Whatever families mean
to each and every one of us
we'll have to admit,

Sometimes it's not always right.

⌘ THE ORANGE BUTTERFLY ⌘

I wanted to look at
all kinds of things
on my walk to the park
as if on a
surveillance.

I had a desire to see a
butterfly, so I looked
up to the sky,
in silence.

In my trainers and sportswear
I walked leisurely.

People,
with their lawnmowers going
up and down as if on marches.
Taking in their stride as they flaunt
their gardens and lawns.

Some, tending to garden and hedges
trimmed down to all shapes and sizes.

Hedges are getting taller to keep
you out, and them in.

Discreetly, I stuck my head in
to take a look, and if I was caught
I'd mark in pleasantries.

At times people looked out of their gardens
and conservatories.

One garden had a theme.
To me it would seem –
'Red Riding Hood',
'Alice in Wonderland' or
'Bill and Ben the Flowerpot
Men'.

A short distance away, something
caught my eye.

I was so sure it would fly,
the moment I was there.

It stood still but the wings
looked clipped.

How wrong was I?

As I stood,
it didn't flinch, flitter or fly.

I wanted to hold the butterfly
in the palm of my hand.

For some reason, I held back
to think it would be contaminated.

I couldn't believe the butterfly came
at the time it did.

I decided to return to the
butterfly, but it had gone
and my heart sank.

When I looked up to the sky
I whispered,
'That was some deliverance'.

And, thanked God.